The God Centered Husband
Bible Study Workbook

GodCenteredFamily.org

God Centered Husband Bible Study Guide
© 2021 GodCenteredFamily.org

No part of this publication may be reproduced, stored in a retrieval system, or transmitted in any form or by any means — electronic, mechanical, photocopy, recording, or any other—except for brief quotations in printed reviews, without the prior permission of the publisher.

Unless otherwise noted, all Scripture quotations are taken from the Christian Standard Bible (Nashville, TN: Holman Bible Publishers, 2020). Used by permission.

*"Husbands, love your wives,
just as Christ loved the church and gave himself for her."*

Ephesians 5:2

Table of Contents

Introduction — 5

Session 1. Genesis 2:15–25 — 8

Session 2. Ephesians 5:22–33 — 14

Session 3. 1 Corinthians 13 — 21

Session 4. 1 Corinthians 7:1–7 — 27

Session 5. Colossians 3:12–19 — 33

Session 6. 1 Peter 3:1–7 — 39

Conclusion — 45

Introduction

What Does It Mean to Be a God Centered Husband?

Every man lives for something.

- Some men live for their career, constantly working to climb the ladder, gain respect, and make a killing.
- Some men live for their wives, passively doing whatever it takes to placate them.
- Most men live for themselves, deciding how to live solely based on what's most comfortable.

Because every husband who reads this is an imperfect husband, we all, to some degree, live for ourselves. This Bible study will challenge you to *stop* living for yourself and live for God instead.

If you're reading this, you probably have some sort of desire to be a good, godly husband. But the only path to becoming the husband that God has called you to be is completely centering your life on *God*, rather than yourself or your wife. Your life doesn't belong to you — you were bought with a price — so stop living for yourself.

God centered husbands live for God and his glory, not themselves. This frees us to lay down our lives in service to our wives.

How to Use This Bible Study

Each lesson in this book will walk through a crucial Bible passage on God's call for husbands. We'll use a Bible study method called S.M.R.T. ("smart") to read, study, understand, and apply each passage. There will be four components to every lesson:

- *What does the text **say**?*
  In this step we read the selected passage, repeatedly and carefully to understand its meaning. Before we can ask questions like "What does this text mean to me?" we have to ask questions like what words are in this passage? What do those words mean? What is the author actually saying?

- *What does the text **mean**?*
  The Bible wasn't written *to* us, so understanding the Bible requires us to understand its original audience. In this step, we'll write a one-sentence summary of this text's meaning to its original audience.

- *What does the text **reveal**?*
  The Bible wasn't written *about* us, it was written about God. The Bible is a revelation of God (literally, a "revealing" of God), so every passage reveals stunning truths about who God is that should cause us to worship him. Because God is unchanging, these timeless truths are also unchanging. In this workbook, we'll also consider timeless truths about God's design for marriage in this section. Because our unchanging God created marriage as an unchanging institution, these timeless truths are also unchanging.

- *What does the text **tell**?*
  When we look at God in his glory through his Word, our lives must be changed. The final step is to understand what the text demands of us, commands us to do, or tells us to do.

This guide can be used alone, one-on-one with another man, or in a small group setting. Before going at it alone, consider inviting another man to join you — someone who will help you apply these principles to your marriage and keep you accountable.

If you choose to go through this Bible study with another guy or a group of guys, keep each other accountable to not complain about your wives. That's off-limits for these conversations (See Philippians 2:14–16).

Next Steps

Every lesson will end with one or two action items for you. This will always include a conversation with your wife and sometimes will include another activity as well.

Don't skip over this. Your wife is invested in your marriage and wants to see you grow as a Christian and as a husband.

Here are a few tips for having these conversations:

- **Don't play defense.** Your wife might point out some pretty painful stuff about your life. This is a gold-mine of action steps to better serve her. Defending yourself is the best way to cut yourself off from this kind of valuable feedback in the future.

- **Be grateful.** When your wife is honest with you, thank her for her honesty (even if it hurts). Proverbs 27:6 says, "The wounds of a friend are trustworthy, but the kisses of an enemy are excessive."

- **Be patient.** If you haven't had this kind of conversation in the past (or if they've gone poorly in the past), understand that it might take time for your wife to open up. Don't force her to talk about anything when she's not ready. If you consistently show up and prove that you're eager to grow, you will earn her trust.

- **Be biblical.** Tell your wife about the things you're learning *and* the passages that you've learned them from. Bring her to God's Word. This is a great way to "wash her in water by the word" (Ephesians 5:26).

Session 1.
Genesis 2:15–25

Today, many secular voices claim that monogamous marriage is a new phenomena — a fairly recent product of evolution. The Bible paints a different picture: marriage isn't a new idea. It's been around since the beginning of time. Our journey to understand how to live as God centered husbands begins by understanding our glorious Creator God and his perfect design for marriage.

This passage is found in the Creation Narrative of Genesis 1–2. It was written by Moses to the Israelites as they were preparing to enter the Promised Land, where they would come face-to-face with many distorted views of the world and of marriage. In the face of a hostile culture, the Israelites needed to be grounded in God's design for marriage, just like us today.

Genesis 2:15–25

15 The LORD God took the man and placed him in the garden of Eden to work it and watch over it. 16 And the LORD God commanded the man, "You are free to eat from any tree of the garden, 17 but you must not eat from the tree of the knowledge of good and evil, for on the day you eat from it, you will certainly die." 18 Then the LORD God said, "It is not good for the man to be alone. I will make a helper corresponding to him." 19 The LORD God formed out of the ground every wild animal and every bird of the sky, and brought each to the man to see what he would call it. And whatever the man called a living creature, that was its name. 20 The man gave names to all the livestock, to the birds of the sky, and to every wild animal; but for the man no helper was found corresponding to him. 21 So the LORD God caused a deep sleep to come over the man, and he slept. God took one of his ribs and closed the flesh at that place. 22 Then the LORD God made the rib he had taken from the man into a woman and brought her to the man. 23 And the man said:

This one, at last, is bone of my bone and flesh of my flesh;

this one will be called "woman," for she was taken from man.

24 This is why a man leaves his father and mother and bonds with his wife, and they become one flesh. 25 Both the man and his wife were naked, yet felt no shame.

Step One. What Does the Text <u>Say</u>?

In this step we read the selected passage, repeatedly and carefully to understand its meaning. There's extra space in between the lines of the passages in this book to give you room for notes, highlights, underlines, squiggly arrows, and any other markings.

- Before picking up your pen, read Genesis 2:15–25 at least twice.
- Circle every reference to God. This includes any names for God and pronouns that refer to God.
- Underline every reference to Adam/the man, including pronouns for the man.
- Find every verb in the passage. Write above each verb who is performing that action.
- Find everywhere in the passage where someone is speaking. Write down who is speaking.
- The word "but" shows contrast — it compares two things that are different. Make a box around the word "but" every time it shows up in the passage (there are two) and write down in the margins what two things are being compared.
- The word "for" often shows reason or grounds — it explains why something took place. Draw a box around the word "for" every time it is used this way in the passage (there are two) and write down what is being described and what reason is given for it.
- There is a slight shift in the text in verse 24. What changes? How would you describe this shift? Make a note in the margin.
- Make notes of any other textual details that stand out to you in the passage.

Step Two. What Does the Text <u>Mean</u>?

In this step, we'll write a one-sentence summary of this text's meaning to its original audience. Do not include any present-day implications or personal applications in this sentence.

Moses wrote to the Israelites to describe how…

_____

_____

_____

Step Three. What Does the Text <u>Reveal</u>?

In this step, we write down the timeless truths that are revealed in this passage. We are focusing on the timeless truths revealed in this passage — things that are true at anytime throughout history and anywhere on the earth. Do not include any present-day implications or personal applications.

<u>What timeless truths about GOD are revealed in this passage?</u>
Try to write down at least five, feel free to write down more if you see them.

1. _____
2. _____
3. _____
4. _____
5. _____

<u>What timeless truths about MARRIAGE are revealed in this passage?</u>
Try to write down at least five, feel free to write down more if you see them.

1. _____
2. _____
3. _____
4. _____
5. _____

Step Four. What Does the Text <u>Tell</u>?

The final step is to understand what the text demands of us, commands us to do, or tells us to do.

Marriage is designed by God. Is your view of your own marriage shaped by God's Word, or your own desires? What truths about marriage from this passage have you struggled to believe in the past? Even if you believe all these truths about marriage in your head, which truths do you struggle to live out in your own marriage?

_____

_____

_____

God said that it wasn't good for Adam to be alone, and when Adam first laid eyes on Eve, he was overwhelmed with joy at what an incredible treasure she was. Your wife is a blessing from God to enjoy. In what ways have you failed to cherish her as the gift that she is?

_____

_____

_____

Verse 24 describes the process of *leaving* one's parents and *cleaving* to one's wife. Is your wife your most significant human relationship? Are there other relationships (or activities) that you are tempted to prioritize above your relationship with your wife?

_____

_____

_____

Verse 25 describes the man and the wife as naked and unashamed. Sex is a glorious gift from God. Do you feel shame around your wife? Why?

_____

_____

_____

How is the text speaking to your marriage? Has God convicted you of any sins to repent of, righteous ways to start, or untrue beliefs to replace? Be specific — what steps will you take?

_____

_____

_____

God is the creator of marriage. He gave a wife to Adam and he gave a wife to you. Pray now, thanking God for your wife and asking him to shape you into the husband he is calling you to be.

Next Steps:
- *Have a conversation with your wife about what you have learned from this passage. Tell her that you cherish her and ask how you can cherish her more.*

Session 2.

Ephesians 5:22–33

Ephesians 5 is one of the most extensive teachings on the husband's role in the entire Bible. This passage explains the great responsibility that husbands have to lovingly serve and lead their wives, just as Christ lovingly serves and leads the church.

Ephesians 5:22–33

22 Wives, submit to your husbands as to the Lord, 23 because the husband is the head of the wife as Christ is the head of the church. He is the Savior of the body. 24 Now as the church submits to Christ, so also wives are to submit to their husbands in everything. 25 Husbands, love your wives, just as Christ loved the church and gave himself for her 26 to make her holy, cleansing her with the washing of water by the word. 27 He did this to present the church to himself in splendor, without spot or wrinkle or anything like that, but holy and blameless. 28 In the same way, husbands are to love their wives as their own bodies. He who loves his wife loves himself. 29 For no one ever hates his own flesh but provides and cares for it, just as Christ does for the church, 30 since we are members of his body. 31 For this reason a man will leave his father and mother and be joined to his wife, and the two will become one flesh. 32 This mystery is profound, but I am talking about Christ and the church. 33 To sum up, each one of you is to love his wife as himself, and the wife is to respect her husband.

> ★ **KEY WORD: Mystery**
>
> A mystery is something with a spiritual meaning that was *once hidden*, but is now revealed. Here in Ephesians 5, Paul says that marriage is a mystery — it's true meaning (a picture of Christ and the church) was once hidden, but is now revealed.

Step One. What Does the Text <u>Say</u>?

In this step we read the selected passage, repeatedly and carefully to understand its meaning. There's extra space in between the lines of the passages in this book to give you room for notes, highlights, underlines, squiggly arrows, and any other markings.

- Before picking up your pen, read Ephesians 5:22–33 at least twice.
- Find every pronoun (e.g., you, he, his, etc.) in the passage and write down who it refers to. Take your time on this one — there are some tricky ones!
- Circle every reference to God. This includes any of the three persons of the Trinity, any names for God, and pronouns that refer to God.
- Draw a box around every reference to husbands, including pronouns that refer to husbands.
- Find every verb in the passage. Write above each verb who is performing that action.
- Make a list of every action that Christ performs in this passage.
- The word "for" often shows reason or grounds — it explains why something took place. Draw a box around the word "for" every time it is used this way in the passage (there are two) and write down what is being described and what reason is given for it.
- Underline every place where husbands are compared to Christ (look for words like "also," "just as," "same," etc.). Are there any other comparisons in this passage?
- Re-read Genesis 2:15–25. Does Ephesians 5 make any reference to Genesis 2? Are there any words or phrases in Ephesians 5 that are taken from Genesis 2? Write "Genesis 2" next to every reference you can find.
- Are there any commands in this passage? Draw a star next to every command and write down who that command is given to.
- Make notes of any other textual details that stand out to you in the passage.

Step Two. What Does the Text **Mean**?

In this step, we'll write a one-sentence summary of this text's meaning to its original audience. Do not include any present-day implications or personal applications in this sentence.

Paul wrote to the Ephesians, teaching them...

_____

_____

_____

Step Three. What Does the Text **Reveal**?

In this step, we write down the timeless truths that are revealed in this passage. We are focusing on the timeless truths revealed in this passage — things that are true at anytime throughout history and anywhere on the earth. Do not include any present-day implications or personal applications.

What timeless truths about GOD are revealed in this passage?
Try to write down at least five, feel free to write down more if you see them.

1. _____
2. _____
3. _____
4. _____
5. _____

What timeless truths about MARRIAGE are revealed in this passage?
Try to write down at least five, feel free to write down more if you see them.

1. _____

2. _____

3. _____

4. _____

5. _____

Step Four. What Does the Text Tell?

The final step is to understand what the text demands of us, commands us to do, or tells us to do.

While the world says that men and women have equal roles, this passage speaks about a husband lovingly serving as the leading head of his wife. Do you believe that God has called you to lovingly lead your wife? What should this leadership look like, according to God's Word?

_____

_____

_____

While the world says that you should make yourself comfortable and compromise with your spouse, this passage speaks about a husband completely laying his life down for his wife. Do you believe that God has called you to lay your life down for your wife? What should this self-sacrifice look like, according to God's Word?

_____

_____

_____

This passage describes Christ cleansing the church by "the washing of water by the word" (v. 26). How do you care for your wife spiritually? Make a plan now to invest in your wife's spiritual growth.

_____
_____
_____

In what ways have you actually sacrificed for your wife in the past week? In what ways have you actually led your wife in the past week?

_____
_____
_____

Which is harder for you: lovingly leading your wife or lovingly sacrificing for your wife? Why? What obstacles (e.g., your own sin, relational dynamics, past circumstances, giftings, etc.) keep you from lovingly leading and lovingly sacrificing for your wife?

_____
_____
_____

What are some practical steps that you can take this week to end your selfishness and sacrifice for your wife? (e.g., plan a date for her, serve her around the house, ask her how you can serve her better, etc.)

_____
_____
_____

What are some practical steps that you can take this week to grow as the leader of your wife? (e.g., practice clear communication, initiate spiritual activities, etc.)

_____

_____

_____

As we read Ephesians 5, we may feel overwhelmed: none of us is the perfect husband. We have all failed to lovingly lead and serve our wives. We are broken husbands, but we are also Christ's bride — he laid down his life for us, cleansing us and making us "holy and blameless."

In Christ's cross and empty tomb, there is grace available for broken husbands like us. Christ also offers the hope and help we need to actually empower us to be the husbands he is calling us to be.

Next Steps:
- *Have a conversation with your wife about what you have learned from this passage. Ask her how you can serve her this week.*
- *Get accountable. Find another man who can help you grow to be the leading, sacrificing husband God that has called you to be.*

Session 3.
1 Corinthians 13

In the last session, we learned about the husband's call to love his wife as Christ loved the church. What does that kind of love look like every day? First Corinthians 13 is a great place to look for that answer.

This chapter comes in the middle of Paul's teaching about the worship of the church. Things were getting pretty crazy in Corinth, where the worship services were overrun with people trying to speak in tongues and prophesy. Paul taught them that it is good to desire these great gifts, but then tells them "I will show you an even better way" (1 Cor 12:31). In 1 Corinthians 13, he describes that love is more important than any impressive spiritual display.

While Paul was teaching about life in a local church, his teachings on love are just as applicable to our own marriages today.

1 Corinthians 13

[1] If I speak human or angelic tongues but do not have love, I am a noisy gong or a clanging cymbal. [2] If I have the gift of prophecy and understand all mysteries and all knowledge, and if I have all faith so that I can move mountains but do not have love, I am nothing. [3] And if I give away all my possessions, and if I give over my body in order to boast but do not have love, I gain nothing. [4] Love is patient, love is kind. Love does not envy, is not boastful, is not arrogant, [5] is not rude, is not self-seeking, is not irritable, and does not keep a record of wrongs. [6] Love finds no joy in unrighteousness but rejoices in the truth. [7] It bears all things, believes all things, hopes all things, endures all things. [8] Love never ends. But as for prophecies, they will come to an end; as for tongues, they will cease; as for knowledge, it will come to an end. [9] For we know in part, and we prophesy in part, [10] but when the perfect comes, the partial will come to an end. [11] When I was a child, I spoke like a child, I thought like a child, I reasoned like a child. When I became a man, I put aside childish things. [12] For now we see only a reflection as in a mirror, but then face to face. Now I know in part, but then I will know fully, as I am fully known. [13] Now these three remain: faith, hope, and love—but the greatest of these is love.

Step One. What Does the Text <u>Say</u>?

In this step we read the selected passage, repeatedly and carefully to understand its meaning. There's extra space in between the lines of the passages in this book to give you room for notes, highlights, underlines, squiggly arrows, and any other markings.

- Before picking up your pen, read 1 Corinthians 13 at least twice.
- Read 1 Corinthians 12. How does that chapter help you understand 1 Corinthians 13:1–3 and 1 Corinthians 13:8–13? Make a summarizing note in the margins.
- The word "but" shows contrast — it compares two things that are different. Make a box around the word "but" every time it shows up in the passage and write down in the margins what two things are being compared.
- Find every pronoun (e.g., it, you, he, his, etc.) in the passage and write down who (or what) it refers to.
- Make a list of every thing that love *is*, according to this passage. If there are any words that you don't know, look them up in a dictionary.
- Make a list of every thing that love *is not*, according to this passage. If there are any words that you don't know, look them up in a dictionary.

Step Two. What Does the Text <u>Mean</u>?

In this step, we'll write a one-sentence summary of this text's meaning to its original audience. Do not include any present-day implications or personal applications in this sentence.

Paul wrote to the Corinthians, teaching them…

_____

_____

_____

Step Three. What Does the Text <u>Reveal</u>?

In this step, we write down the timeless truths that are revealed in this passage. We are focusing on the timeless truths revealed in this passage — things that are true at anytime throughout history and anywhere on the earth. Do not include any present-day implications or personal applications.

<u>What timeless truths about GOD are revealed in this passage?</u>
God's name is obviously not mentioned in this passage, but "God is love" (1 John 4:8), which means that he perfectly displays all of the characteristics of love.

Pick at least five of the attributes of love from this passage and describe how God exhibits them. Feel free to write down more than five.

1. _____

2. _____

3. _____

4. _____

5. _____

Step Four. What Does the Text <u>Tell</u>?
The final step is to understand what the text demands of us, commands us to do, or tells us to do.

In what ways have you valued other religious activities and performances above love for your wife (cf. vv. 1–3)?

_____

_____

_____

Which attribute of love have you struggled to show in your marriage? What do you think has kept you from loving your wife in this way?

_____

_____

_____

What practical steps will you take to grow in that attribute of love?

_____

_____

_____

Which of the negative attributes of love (the things that love *is not*) is most prominent in your marriage? In what ways does it show up?

_____

_____

_____

What practical steps will you take to put to death that negative attribute of love?

_____

_____

_____

Love is not a choice for Christians. When we fail to love our wives, we are failing to represent the relationship between Christ and the church.
You could never work up enough love on your own, because love is a fruit of the Spirit (Galatians 5:22). This means that God the Holy Spirit can (and will!) bring it about in your life.

Pray now, asking God to fill you up with this kind of love for your wife, and others.

Next Steps:
- *Have a conversation with your wife about what you have learned from this passage. Share your lists of what love is and is not with her and ask her how she would like to see you grow.*

Session 4.
1 Corinthians 7:1–7

As a husband, you are to love your wife in every area of your marriage. How does this kind of Christ-imaging, self-denying love inform the way we think about sex? First Corinthians 7 gives us an answer.

The church at Corinth was an absolute mess, and some people had started falsely teaching the church "It is good for a man to not have sexual relations with a woman." Paul refutes this false teaching and offers godly wisdom for enjoying sex as a gift from God for husbands and wives.

1 Corinthians 7:1–7

[1] Now in response to the matters you wrote about: "It is good for a man not to have sexual relations with a woman." [2] But because sexual immorality is so common, each man should have sexual relations with his own wife, and each woman should have sexual relations with her own husband. [3] A husband should fulfill his marital duty to his wife, and likewise a wife to her husband. [4] A wife does not have the right over her own body, but her husband does. In the same way, a husband does not have the right over his own body, but his wife does. [5] Do not deprive one another—except when you agree for a time, to devote yourselves to prayer. Then come together again; otherwise, Satan may tempt you because of your lack of self-control. [6] I say this as a concession, not as a command. [7] I wish that all people were as I am. But each has his own gift from God, one person has this gift, another has that.

Step One. What Does the Text <u>Say</u>?

In this step we read the selected passage, repeatedly and carefully to understand its meaning. There's extra space in between the lines of the passages in this book to give you room for notes, highlights, underlines, squiggly arrows, and any other markings.

- Before picking up your pen, read 1 Corinthians 7:1–7 at least twice.
- Find every pronoun (e.g., you, he, his, etc.) in the passage and write down who it refers to.
- Circle every reference to God. This includes any of the three persons of the Trinity, any names for God, and pronouns that refer to God.
- Draw a box around every reference to husbands, including pronouns that refer to husbands.
- There is a quote in verse one. Who said this quote? Write down the speaker in the margins above or below the quote.
- The word "but" shows contrast — it compares two things that are different. Make a box around the word "but" every time it shows up in the passage and write down in the margins what two things are being compared.
- The word "because" often shows reason or grounds — it explains why something took place. Draw a box around the word "because" is used this way in the passage (there are two) and write down what is being described and what reason is given for it.
- Are there any commands in this passage? Draw a star next to every command and write down who that command is given to.
- Make notes of any other textual details that stand out to you in the passage.

Step Two. What Does the Text <u>Mean</u>?

In this step, we'll write a one-sentence summary of this text's meaning to its original audience. Do not include any present-day implications or personal applications in this sentence.

Paul wrote to the Corinthians, teaching them…

_____

_____

_____

Step Three. What Does the Text <u>Reveal</u>?

In this step, we write down the timeless truths that are revealed in this passage. We are focusing on the timeless truths revealed in this passage — things that are true at anytime throughout history and anywhere on the earth. Do not include any present-day implications or personal applications.

<u>What timeless truths about GOD are revealed in this passage?</u>
Try to write down at least five, feel free to write down more if you see them.

1. _____
2. _____
3. _____
4. _____
5. _____

<u>What timeless truths about MARRIAGE are revealed in this passage?</u>
Try to write down at least five, feel free to write down more if you see them.

1. _____
2. _____
3. _____
4. _____
5. _____

Step Four. What Does the Text <u>Tell</u>?

The final step is to understand what the text demands of us, commands us to do, or tells us to do.

The Corinthians were believing that sex was a bad thing to be avoided. In contrast, Paul offers a generally positive view of sex. Do you view sex as a positive thing to be enjoyed between a husband and wife or a negative thing to be avoided (e.g., do you feel shameful about your body, scared of sex, etc.)? If not, what other ways is your view of sex shaped by the world instead of the Bible?

_____

_____

_____

Read verses 3–5 again. What responsibilities does each spouse have in sex?

_____

_____

_____

Husbands have a duty to love their wives during sex (see Ephesians 5:28–30). In what ways have you failed to self-sacrificially loved your wife during sex?

_____

_____

_____

This passage makes clear that sex is to be a *regular* part of Christian marriages. Instead of using this as an excuse to make demands of your wife (see Romans 15:1–3), use this as a command to pursue your wife. What steps can you take to pursue your wife sexually this week, without expecting anything in return?

_____

_____

_____

Practically, do you know how to please your wife sexually (both physically and emotionally)? Have a conversation with your wife and ask her how you can serve her better sexually. Write down her tips here:

_____

_____

_____

Like the Corinthians, we are surrounded with false teaching and bad ideas about sex. First Corinthians 7 gives us a radical, countercultural call to serve our wives sexually. Instead of using sex as an activity to seek maximum satisfaction for yourself, seek maximum satisfaction for your wife.

We don't always insist on getting our own way — we love our wives with a cross-shaped love that allows us deny ourselves to serve them.

Next Steps:
- *Have a conversation with your wife about what you have learned from this passage. Ask her how you can better serve her sexually. It takes a lot of humility to ask your wife, "What can I do to make you feel good in bed?" But this will lead to incredible fruit in your marriage.*

Session 5.
Colossians 3:12–19

In his letter to the Colossians, Paul explains how the resurrection of Christ transforms every area of the Christians life. This applies to every one of our human relationships, including our marriage.

Colossians 3:12–19

12 Therefore, as God's chosen ones, holy and dearly loved, put on compassion, kindness, humility, gentleness, and patience, 13 bearing with one another and forgiving one another if anyone has a grievance against another. Just as the Lord has forgiven you, so you are also to forgive. 14 Above all, put on love, which is the perfect bond of unity. 15 And let the peace of Christ, to which you were also called in one body, rule your hearts. And be thankful. 16 Let the word of Christ dwell richly among you, in all wisdom teaching and admonishing one another through psalms, hymns, and spiritual songs, singing to God with gratitude in your hearts. 17 And whatever you do, in word or in deed, do everything in the name of the Lord Jesus, giving thanks to God the Father through him. 18 Wives, submit yourselves to your husbands, as is fitting in the Lord. 19 Husbands, love your wives and don't be bitter toward them.

Step One. What Does the Text <u>Say</u>?

In this step we read the selected passage, repeatedly and carefully to understand its meaning. There's extra space in between the lines of the passages in this book to give you room for notes, highlights, underlines, squiggly arrows, and any other markings.

- Before picking up your pen, read Colossians 3:12-19 at least twice. Read Colossians 3:19 at least ten times.
- Find every pronoun (e.g., you, he, his, etc.) in the passage and write down who it refers to.
- Who is this passage addressed to (v. 12)? What does it mean to be "God's chosen ones?"
- If there are any words in the passage that you can't define, look them up in a dictionary and copy down the definition.
- Draw a box around words that indicate a comparison ("and," "but," "as," "so," etc.) and write down what is being described and what reason is given for it.
- Are there any commands in this passage? Draw a star next to every command and write down who that command is given to.
- In verse 19, husbands are commanded to not "be bitter" toward their wives. Some translations say "do not be harsh with them" (e.g., ESV). This word (Greek, πικραίνω) is used four times in the New Testament (Colossians 3:19; Revelation 8:11, 10:9, 10:10). Read the other uses and come up with a working definition.
- Make notes of any other textual details that stand out to you in the passage.

Step Two. What Does the Text <u>Mean</u>?

In this step, we'll write a one-sentence summary of this text's meaning to its original audience. Do not include any present-day implications or personal applications in this sentence.

Paul wrote to the Colossians, teaching them...

_____

_____

_____

Step Three. What Does the Text <u>Reveal</u>?

In this step, we write down the timeless truths that are revealed in this passage. We are focusing on the timeless truths revealed in this passage — things that are true at anytime throughout history and anywhere on the earth. Do not include any present-day implications or personal applications.

<u>What timeless truths about GOD are revealed in this passage?</u>
Try to write down at least five, feel free to write down more if you see them.

1. _____
2. _____
3. _____
4. _____
5. _____

<u>What timeless truths about MARRIAGE are revealed in this passage?</u>
Try to write down at least five, feel free to write down more if you see them.

1. _____
2. _____
3. _____
4. _____
5. _____

Step Four. What Does the Text <u>Tell</u>?

The final step is to understand what the text demands of us, commands us to do, or tells us to do.

This passage is addressed to "God's Chosen Ones" and the grounds of our forgiveness of others is God's forgiveness of us. Do you believe that God has forgiven you? What steps do you take to remind yourself of God's grace every day?

_____

_____

_____

Paul describes love as "the perfect bond of unity." Think back to your study in 1 Corinthians 13. Revisit the attributes of love that you most wanted to improve in your own marriage. How have you been doing in those areas? How will continuing to improve in those areas bring more unity to your marriage?

_____

_____

_____

In what ways have you allowed bitterness to enter your marriage? Common answers are unforgiveness, lack of grace for your wife's mistakes, lack of mercy for your wife's weaknesses, and a harsh, demanding spirit.

_____

_____

_____

Re-read Colossians 3:13 and then read Matthew 18:21–35. How will remembering that God has forgiven you help you forgive your wife?

_____

_____

_____

Are you harboring unforgiveness or resentment against your wife? What practical steps will you take to end it?

_____

_____

_____

The self-centered husband gets angry whenever his wife sins or makes a mistake. The God centered husband forgives his wife, knowing how greatly he's been forgiven by God.

Next Steps:
- *Have a conversation with your wife. Ask her if there are any areas where your actions, demands, or words have been harsh. Repent, asking for her forgiveness*

Session 6.
1 Peter 3:1–7

Peter wrote this letter to "Elect Exiles" (1:1), people of God who are living in the midst of a hostile world. Their primary identity was not citizens of the Roman Empire, but citizens of the Kingdom of God. Peter encouraged his readers to live a God centered life, because they are a part of a God centered Kingdom. This radical God centered orientation informs every area of their lives, including marriage.

1 Peter 3:1–7

¹ In the same way, wives, submit yourselves to your own husbands so that, even if some disobey the word, they may be won over without a word by the way their wives live ² when they observe your pure, reverent lives. ³ Don't let your beauty consist of outward things like elaborate hairstyles and wearing gold jewelry or fine clothes, ⁴ but rather what is inside the heart,—the imperishable quality of a gentle and quiet spirit, which is of great worth in God's sight. ⁵ For in the past, the holy women who put their hope in God also adorned themselves in this way, submitting to their own husbands, ⁶ just as Sarah obeyed Abraham, calling him lord. You have become her children when you do what is good and do not fear any intimidation. ⁷ Husbands, in the same way, live with your wives in an understanding way, as with a weaker partner, showing them honor as coheirs of the grace of life, so that your prayers will not be hindered.

Step One. What Does the Text <u>Say</u>?

In this step we read the selected passage, repeatedly and carefully to understand its meaning. There's extra space in between the lines of the passages in this book to give you room for notes, highlights, underlines, squiggly arrows, and any other markings.

- Before picking up your pen, read 1 Peter 3:1–7 at least twice.
- Find every pronoun (e.g., you, he, his, etc.) in the passage and write down who it refers to.
- Are there any commands in this passage? Draw a star next to every command and write down who that command is given to.
- The word "but" shows contrast — it compares two things that are different. Make a box around the word "but" every time it shows up in the passage and write down in the margins what two things are being compared.
- The word "for" often shows reason or grounds — it explains why something took place. Draw a box around the word "for" every time it is used this way in the passage and write down what is being described and what reason is given for it.
- What does Peter mean in verse seven by the phrase "in the same way?" How are his commands for husbands similar to his commands for wives?
- What do you think it means for husbands and wives to be "coheirs of the grace of life" (see Galatians 4:1–7)?
- The phrase "so that" shows an expected result — it explains what will happen if a certain action is taken. Draw a box around the phrase "so that" is used this way in the passage and write down what is being described and what reason is given for it.
- If there are any words in the passage that you can't define, look them up in a dictionary and copy down the definition.
- Make notes of any other textual details that stand out to you in the passage.

Step Two. What Does the Text **Mean**?

In this step, we'll write a one-sentence summary of this text's meaning to its original audience. Do not include any present-day implications or personal applications in this sentence.

Peter wrote to the churches of Asia, teaching them...

_____

_____

_____

Step Three. What Does the Text **Reveal**?

In this step, we write down the timeless truths that are revealed in this passage. We are focusing on the timeless truths revealed in this passage — things that are true at anytime throughout history and anywhere on the earth. Do not include any present-day implications or personal applications.

What timeless truths about GOD are revealed in this passage?
Try to write down at least five, feel free to write down more if you see them.

1. _____

2. _____

3. _____

4. _____

5. _____

<u>What timeless truths about MARRIAGE are revealed in this passage?</u>
Try to write down at least five, feel free to write down more if you see them.

1. _____
2. _____
3. _____
4. _____
5. _____

Step Four. What Does the Text <u>Tell</u>?

The final step is to understand what the text demands of us, commands us to do, or tells us to do.

Peter encourages wives to have a "gentle and quiet spirit" (v. 4), and then instructs husbands to serve their wives "in the same way." What are some ways that can practically be more gentle with your wife?

_____

_____

_____

In what ways have you not lived with your wife in an understanding way? Are you impatient with her weaknesses, unforgiving of her sins, or overly harsh and critical?

_____

_____

_____

When was the last time you publicly *honored* your wife? How can you make a habit of honoring your wife privately and publicly?

_____

_____

_____

Peter warns harsh husbands that their prayers will be hindered. Write a short prayer of repentance, asking God to forgive you for your lack of understanding. Appeal to God's mercy for your lack of mercy.

_____

_____

_____

Most husbands can easily rattle off a list of things they don't like about their wives. Can you make a list of praiseworthy things about your wife? Write down ten right now. Make a habit of praising your wife every day.

1. _____

2. _____

3. _____

4. _____

5. _____

6. _____

7. _____

8. _____

9. _____

10. _____

By grace, we live the God centered life to serve and support our wives. As we do this, we are showing our wives (and the watching world) a stunning picture of Christ serving the church.

This task is not to be taken lightly. We need God's help every step of the way. And the good news is *we have his help*. In his death and resurrection, Christ has purchased God's grace for us. We have every grace we need to obey his commands and imitate his love.

Husbands, love your wives as Christ loved the church.
Husbands, love your wives *because* Christ loved you.

Next Steps:
- *Have a conversation with your wife about what you learned in this passage and in this study as a whole. Ask her how you can grow as a spiritual leader.*
- *Pick one of the passages in this book and memorize it.*

Conclusion

Living the God Centered Life

Every man lives for something. My hope and prayer is that this Bible study workbook has challenged you, encouraged you, and equipped you to live for God.

If you are looking for more resources to help you lead your wife and children, I hope you'll check out the resources at GodCenteredFamily.org.

If you subscribe to GodCenteredFamily.org, you'll receive everything you need for a daily family devotion, so you can teach your kids the truth about God in just ten minutes a day. And if your wife is a Christian, she will probably be THRILLED to see you taking this initiative to disciple her and your kids.

I hope you'll continue to radically serve your wife.
I hope you'll continue to cling to Christ, who has radically served you.

"In the same way, husbands are to love their wives as their own bodies. He who loves his wife loves himself. For no one ever hates his own flesh but provides and cares for it, **just as Christ does for the church***...." (Ephesians 5:28–29)*

Printed by Amazon Italia Logistica S.r.l.
Torrazza Piemonte (TO), Italy